D1416385

THE GREATEST RECORDS IN SPORTS
SOCCER'S
GREATEST RECORDS

Emily Jankowski

PowerKiDS press

New York

Published in 2015 by The Rosen Publishing Group, Inc.
29 East 21st Street, New York, NY 10010

First Edition

Editor: Katie Kawa
Book Design: Mickey Harmon

Photo Credits: Cover (stadium) EKS/Shutterstock.com; cover (Beckham) Richard Wolowicz/Stringer/Getty Images Sport/Getty Images; cover (Hamm) Al Messerschmidt/Staff/Getty Images; p. 5 Thorsten Wagner/Stringer/Bongarts/Getty Images; pp. 7, 14 Photo Works/Shutterstock.com; p. 9 Allen Kee/Stringer/Getty Images; p. 11 Thearon W. Henderson/Stringer/Getty Images; p. 13 Jamie Sabau/Stringer/Getty Images Sport/Getty Images; p. 15 HARRY S. CAHILL/Staff/Getty Images; p. 16 Mike Hewitt - FIFA/Contributor/Getty Images; pp. 17, 20 AGIF/Shutterstock.com; p. 19 Art Rickerby/Contributor/The LIFE Picture Collection/Getty Images; p. 21 http://upload.wikimedia.org/wikipedia/commons/9/9d/Football_against_poverty_2014_-_Ronaldo.jpg p. 23 Martin Rose/Staff/Getty Images Sport/Getty Images; p. 25 The Asahi Shimbun/Contributor/Getty Images; p. 27 Grant Halverson/Contributor/Getty Images; p. 28 Rick Stewart/Stringer/Getty Images Sport/Getty Images; p. 29 Jared Wickerham/Staff/Getty Images; p. 30 Fotokostic/Shutterstock.com.

Library of Congress Cataloging-in-Publication Data

Jankowski, Emily.
Soccer's greatest records / by Emily Jankowski.
p. cm. — (The greatest records in sports)
Includes index.
ISBN 978-1-4994-0001-4 (pbk.)
ISBN 978-1-4994-0002-1 (6-pack)
ISBN 978-1-4994-0000-7 (library binding)
1. Soccer — Records — Juvenile literature. 2. Major League Soccer (Organization) — Juvenile literature. I. Jankowski, Emily. II. Title.
GV943.4 J36 2015
796.334—d23

Manufactured in the United States of America

CPSIA Compliance Information: Batch #CW15PK: For Further Information contact Rosen Publishing, New York, New York at 1-800-237-9932

CONTENTS

THE WORLD'S GAME

Soccer has been called the "world's game" because of its growing popularity around the world. It's a sport played by two teams of 11 players each with a round ball that may not be touched with the hands or arms during play, except by the goalies. The object of the game is to score goals by kicking or heading the ball into the other team's goal.

Games similar to soccer have been around for hundreds of years. The beginning of soccer as we know it can be traced back to England in 1863. Since that time, many **statistics**—also called stats—have been used to measure the success of teams and players. Around the world, there are different leagues and **tournaments** that teams compete in, and each has its own records. In the United States, the men's **professional** league is called Major League Soccer (MLS).

Long before soccer as we know it today was played in England, similar games were played in ancient China.

GOAL!

A goal in soccer is scored when a player uses any part of their body (other than their arms or hands) to put the soccer ball in the net. Soccer is a low-scoring sport, and it's not uncommon to have only one goal scored in the entire 90-minute game, or match. This means that when a goal is scored, it's very exciting for the scoring team and its fans!

A forward (sometimes called a striker) is a kind of soccer player who commonly scores the most goals. Having a record for scoring the most goals is a big accomplishment many players **aspire** to. The record for most career MLS goals is currently held by Landon Donovan, who is one of the most famous players in U.S. soccer history.

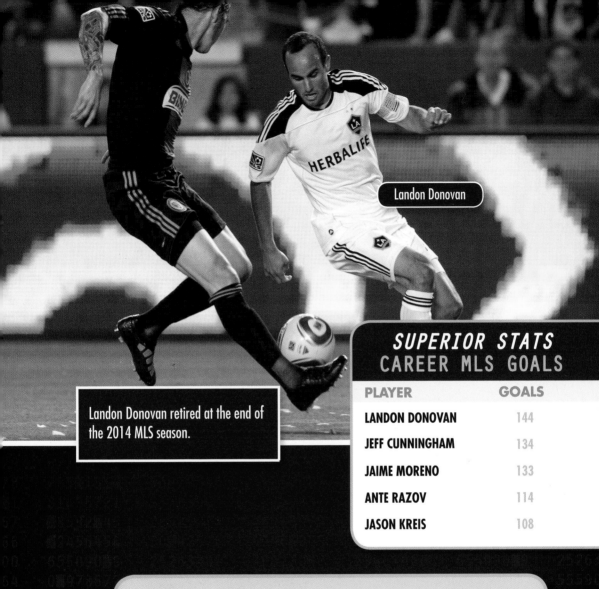

Landon Donovan

Landon Donovan retired at the end of the 2014 MLS season.

SUPERIOR STATS
CAREER MLS GOALS

PLAYER	GOALS
LANDON DONOVAN	144
JEFF CUNNINGHAM	134
JAIME MORENO	133
ANTE RAZOV	114
JASON KREIS	108

LANDON DONOVAN
(1982–)

Landon Donovan is the all-time MLS scoring leader. He was born in Ontario, California, and he began playing **competitive** soccer when he was five years old. Donovan joined the U.S. national soccer program in his last year of high school. He also holds the U.S. Men's National Team (USMNT) record for scoring, with 57 goals.

HELPING THE FORWARDS

Assists are important soccer plays, too. If a player has an assist, it means they passed the ball to the player who scored a goal. No more than two players can be **awarded** an assist on one goal.

Any player on the team—regardless of the position they play—can get an assist. They just have to be one of the last two people to touch the ball before passing it to the scorer. In fact, even a goalie could have an assist! Sometimes, no one is credited with an assist on a goal. This happens if the goal scorer **dribbles** through many defenders or can't find a teammate to pass the ball to.

STEVE RALSTON
(1974–)

Steve Ralston started playing in the MLS in 1996. He's second behind Donovan on the list of most career MLS assists. Ralston is currently retired, but he's now a coach, helping other MLS players **achieve** greatness. He's currently an assistant coach for the Houston Dynamo.

SUPERIOR STATS
CAREER MLS ASSISTS

PLAYER	ASSISTS
LANDON DONOVAN	136
STEVE RALSTON	135
CARLOS VALDERRAMA	114
PREKI	112
BRAD DAVIS	106

Steve Ralston

In order to become MLS record holders for assists, Steve Ralston and Landon Donovan worked hard perfecting their passing skills.

GOALKEEPING RECORDS

A goalie, or goalkeeper, stands in front of the net and tries to keep players on the **opposing** team from scoring. The goalie is the only player on the team who's allowed to use their hands.

Goalies often train in different ways than other players, because their job is very different. They don't generally need to practice dribbling or passes. In fact, many goalies have their own coach to teach them how to make saves.

When a team wins a match, its goalie records a stat called a win. To have the record for wins, a goalie must have a long and successful career, commonly with a good team. Kevin Hartman holds the MLS wins record, with 180 in his career.

SUPERIOR STATS
CAREER MLS WINS

PLAYER	WINS
KEVIN HARTMAN	180
NICK RIMANDO*	163
ZACH THORNTON	131
JOE CANNON	119
MATT REIS	110
JON BUSCH*	110

* = active player

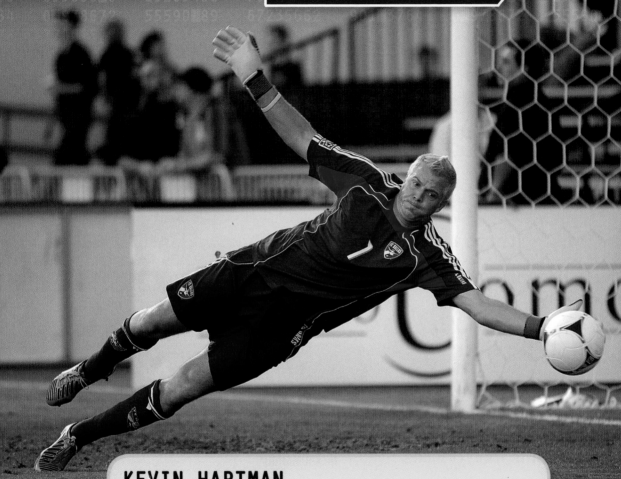

Hartman currently holds the MLS wins record. However, the player behind him on that list, Nick Rimando, is still playing. He might break Hartman's record someday!

KEVIN HARTMAN

(1974–)

Kevin Hartman holds the record for the most career MLS wins. Hartman started playing in the MLS in 1997, and he retired in 2013. He's currently the only player in MLS history to start over 400 regular-season games, but that could change as more players continue their careers.

A shutout is a big accomplishment for a goalie. If a goalie gets a shutout, it means the other team scored no goals.

Shutouts are often made possible by the help a goalie receives from their defenders. Defenders are the players whose position is in front of their own net, and their job is to keep the other team out of that area.

Rimando currently holds the MLS record for most shutouts, which was once held by Hartman. His number of shutouts could continue to rise even higher as he keeps playing. A goalie with a long career will often have more shutouts than goalies who played for a shorter period of time.

SUPERIOR STATS
CAREER MLS SHUTOUTS

PLAYER	SHUTOUTS
NICK RIMANDO*	114
KEVIN HARTMAN	112
JOE CANNON	86
JON BUSCH*	82
ZACH THORNTON	76

* = active player

A goalie has a very high-pressure job. If a goalie makes one mistake, it could end up costing their team the game. The best goalies in soccer handle that kind of pressure well.

THE MLS CUP

Playoff games are held to determine which MLS team is the best. All MLS teams play 34 games throughout the regular season. At the end of the season, the top 10 teams with the most points compete in a series of playoff games.

Matches can end in ties during the regular season, but not in the playoffs. If teams are tied after 90 minutes, they play two 15-minute overtime periods. If they're still tied, they go to penalty kicks, where five players from each team take turns shooting at the opposing goalie. Whichever team scores on the most penalty kicks wins.

DAVID BECKHAM
(1975–)

David Beckham is one of soccer's most popular stars. Although he's from England and began playing soccer in Europe, he played for the Los Angeles Galaxy starting in 2007. Beckham was part of the MLS Cup-winning Galaxy teams in 2011 and 2012. Beckham was a midfielder, which is a position between the forwards and defense. He retired from professional soccer in 2013.

D.C. United won the first MLS Cup in 1996. Beckham won his first MLS Cup 15 years after that.

The two most successful teams in the MLS playoffs are the Los Angeles Galaxy and D.C. United. They've each won four MLS Cups. The MLS Cup is the name for the MLS championship game.

SUPERIOR STATS
MOST MLS CUPS
(AS OF THE 2013 SEASON)

TEAM	MLS CUPS	YEARS WON
LOS ANGELES GALAXY	4	2002, 2005, 2011, 2012
D.C. UNITED	4	1996, 1997, 1999, 2004
HOUSTON DYNAMO	2	2006, 2007
SPORTING KANSAS CITY	2	2000, 2013
SAN JOSE EARTHQUAKES	2	2001, 2003

"FIFA" stands for the French words "Fédération Internationale de Football Association." It's the organization that governs **international** soccer matches. The FIFA World Cup is a major international tournament that happens once every two years. Men and women each have their own World Cup. The men's and women's tournaments each happen once every four years.

LIONEL MESSI
(1987–)

Lionel Messi was born in Argentina and has been named FIFA's Player of the Year a record four times in a row! In 2014, he won the Golden Ball, a prize given to the best player in the World Cup. Even though Argentina lost the final match to Germany, people still thought Messi was the best player throughout the tournament.

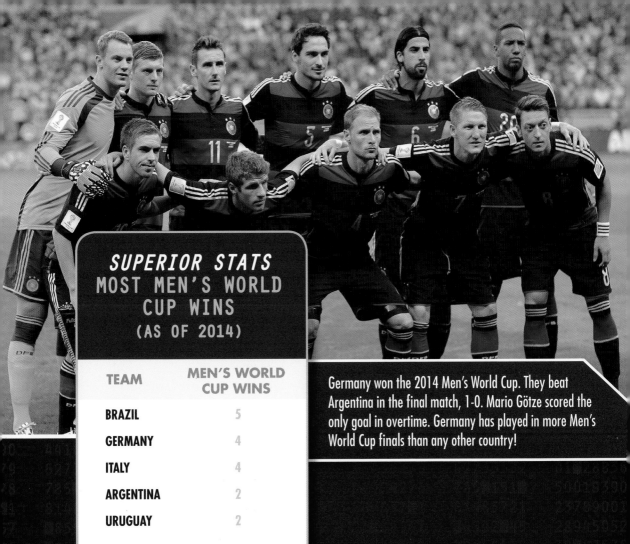

SUPERIOR STATS
MOST MEN'S WORLD
CUP WINS
(AS OF 2014)

TEAM	MEN'S WORLD CUP WINS
BRAZIL	5
GERMANY	4
ITALY	4
ARGENTINA	2
URUGUAY	2

Germany won the 2014 Men's World Cup. They beat Argentina in the final match, 1-0. Mario Götze scored the only goal in overtime. Germany has played in more Men's World Cup finals than any other country!

In order to qualify for the World Cup, a country forms a national team and plays in qualifying tournaments and **preliminary** matches. Only 32 countries qualify. Traditionally, Brazil, Germany, Argentina, and Italy have very strong teams at the Men's World Cup. Brazil holds the record for most Men's World Cup wins, with five.

17

Only the best players are chosen to represent their country in the World Cup. Many countries, including the United States, have programs that train young players to try out for their national team. Once a player makes the team, they must continue to work hard and improve their skills, because there are many other players who are willing to take their place.

It's a huge accomplishment to play in the World Cup as a young player, because younger players don't have as much experience as older players. As of 2014, the youngest players in Men's World Cup history were all 17 years old. One of the youngest, Pelé, went on to become one of the greatest World Cup players in the history of the tournament.

PELÉ
(1940–)

Pelé (whose full name is Edson Arantes do Nascimento) is considered to be one of the best soccer players of all time. He was born in Brazil and became a superstar during the 1958 World Cup. Pelé won the World Cup three times, more than any other player. He's also responsible for helping soccer become a more popular sport in the 1970s.

Pelé

Pelé played a huge role in Brazil's record-setting number of World Cup wins. He was on three of the five teams that won the tournament for Brazil.

SUPERIOR STATS
YOUNGEST PLAYERS IN THE MEN'S WORLD CUP

PLAYER	COUNTRY	WORLD CUP YEAR	AGE
NORMAN WHITESIDE	NORTHERN IRELAND	1982	17 YEARS, 1 MONTH, 10 DAYS
SAMUEL ETOO	CAMEROON	1988	17 YEARS, 3 MONTHS, 7 DAYS
FEMI OPABUNMI	NIGERIA	2002	17 YEARS, 3 MONTHS, 9 DAYS
SALOMON OLEMBE	CAMEROON	1998	17 YEARS, 6 MONTHS, 3 DAYS
PELÉ	BRAZIL	1958	17 YEARS, 7 MONTHS, 23 DAYS

THE WORLD'S BEST PLAYERS

There are many rounds to the World Cup tournament. First, countries must play qualifying games before they even get to the World Cup. Once they make it into the tournament, they first face a round called group play. This round features eight groups of four teams each, and each team plays against the other three teams in their group. The top two teams from each group move on to the knockout stage, where teams are **eliminated** if they lose.

It's difficult enough to score a goal in soccer, but when you are up against the best goalkeepers in the world, it's even harder. The record for most World Cup goals in a career is 16, which was set by Germany's Miroslav Klose.

Miroslav Klose

RONALDO (1976–)

Born in Brazil in 1976, Ronaldo Luís Nazário led his home country to the World Cup title in 2000. He retired in 2011 as one of soccer's greatest players and second behind Klose for most World Cup goals. He also helped organize Brazil's 2014 World Cup.

SUPERIOR STATS
MOST CAREER WORLD CUP GOALS
(AS OF 2014)

PLAYER	COUNTRY	WORLD CUP GOALS
MIROSLAV KLOSE	GERMANY	16
RONALDO	BRAZIL	15
GERD MUELLER	GERMANY	14
JUST FONTAINE	FRANCE	13
PELÉ	BRAZIL	12

One of the most exciting events in the World Cup is a penalty kick shootout. This occurs when two teams are tied at the end of the 90-minute match. If the teams are still tied after two 15-minute overtime periods, the game is decided by penalty kicks. Each team must choose five of their players to go head-to-head with the other team's goalie.

A coin toss determines which country shoots first. Players must shoot one at a time, and players from each country **alternate** shooting and goalkeeping. Each player can only shoot once. This is very exciting, because the whole game comes down to just a few minutes of players going head-to-head against each other. As of the 2014 World Cup, Argentina holds the record for most World Cup shootouts played, with five.

SO MANY SHOOTOUTS

The record for the most penalty kick shootouts in one World Cup is four. This record was set in 1990 when the World Cup was played in Italy. The 2006 World Cup in Germany also had four shootouts. Brazil's 2014 World Cup tied the record, too.

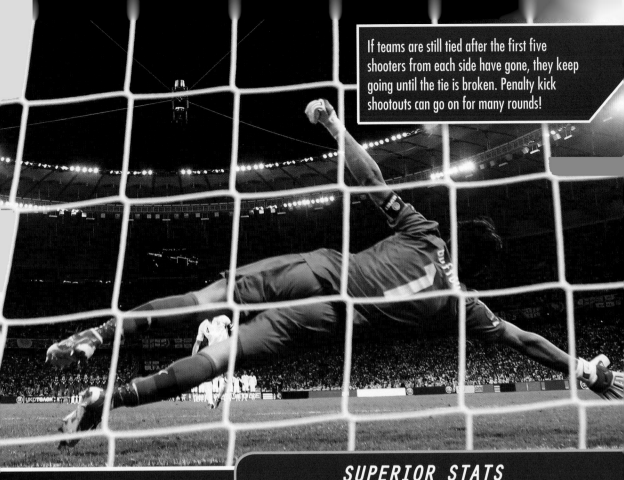

If teams are still tied after the first five shooters from each side have gone, they keep going until the tie is broken. Penalty kick shootouts can go on for many rounds!

SUPERIOR STATS
MOST WORLD CUP
PENALTY KICK SHOOTOUTS
(AS OF 2014)

COUNTRY	SHOOTOUTS	SHOOTOUT WINS
ARGENTINA	5	4
GERMANY	4	4
BRAZIL	4	3
FRANCE	4	2
ITALY	4	1

OLYMPIC SOCCER

Soccer is a sport at the Summer Olympics, which occur every four years. Both men and women compete in separate tournaments during each Summer Olympics.

Men's soccer was added to the list of Olympic sports in 1900. Women's soccer wasn't added to the Olympics until 1996. Although the World Cup is generally seen as the most famous tournament in soccer, it's still an honor to win a medal at the Olympics. The best players from each country also compete against each other at the Olympics.

Hungary holds the record for most total Olympic medals for men's soccer, with five as of the 2012 London Olympics. Hungary is also tied with Great Britain for the most gold medals. As of the 2012 Olympics, both countries have won three gold medals.

AFRICA'S OLYMPIC SUCCESS

Soccer is a very popular sport throughout Africa, and that continent has produced many great players, especially in recent years. In 1996, Nigeria became the first African country to win an Olympic gold medal for men's soccer. In 2000, Cameroon kept the gold in Africa when they won.

Every four years, countries have a chance to break Olympic soccer records.

SUPERIOR STATS
MOST OLYMPIC MEN'S SOCCER MEDALS
(AS OF 2012)

COUNTRY	GOLD MEDALS	TOTAL MEDALS
HUNGARY	3	5
GREAT BRITAIN	3	3
ARGENTINA	2	4
SOVIET UNION	2	5
URUGUAY	2	2

The U.S. Women's National Team (USWNT) gives female soccer players from all over the country the opportunity to showcase their talents. There's also a women's professional league, called the National Women's Soccer League (NWSL).

Women's soccer players have been role models for young female athletes in the United States for many years. Former players, such as Mia Hamm, Julie Foudy, and Kristine Lilly, helped the USWNT grow into the championship-winning team it is today. Current stars, such as Abby Wambach, Alex Morgan, and Christine Rampone, continue to set new records. Wambach has scored more goals in her international career than any other male or female soccer player, and she's still playing! Her record number of goals will continue to increase.

Abby Wambach

The USWNT holds the record for most Olympic gold medals in women's soccer, with four as of 2012. Wambach has two gold medals, winning them in 2004 and 2012.

ABBY WAMBACH
(1980–)

Abby Wambach is the youngest of seven children, so it's easy to see where her toughness comes from! That toughness has helped her score a record-breaking number of goals. Wambach is a forward for the Western New York Flash of the NWSL.

SUPERIOR STATS
MOST USWNT GOALS

PLAYER	GOALS
ABBY WAMBACH*	170
MIA HAMM	158
KRISTINE LILLY	130
MICHELLE AKERS	105
TIFFENY MILBRETT	100

* = active player

The USWNT has been successful in many tournaments, including the Olympics and the Women's World Cup. Perhaps the most memorable moment for U.S. women's soccer was during the 1999 World Cup, when the final against China went into overtime and then a shootout. Brandi Chastain scored during penalty kicks to lead the U.S. to victory, in front of a record TV audience and over 90,000 people in the stands in California.

The USWNT has also been very successful at the Olympics. In fact, the team has won a medal in every Olympics in which they've competed.

MIA HAMM
(1972–)

Mia Hamm played with the USWNT for 17 years, won the World Cup in 1991 and 1999, and won gold medals at the Olympics in 1996 and 2004. She holds the record for career assists in women's soccer, with 144. She's also second on the list of all-time scorers, with 158 goals.

The win at the 1999 World Cup gave a huge boost to the popularity of women's soccer in the United States. The players from that team paved the way for today's female soccer stars and record holders.

The record holders in women's soccer have become the most popular U.S. female athletes of their time. They've helped female athletes in all sports gain more popularity and more respect.

Many people believe soccer is so popular because it can be played almost anywhere. Children around the world grow up playing soccer with neighborhood friends or at school.

The United States has taken a growing interest in soccer in the past few decades, especially since the Women's World Cup in 1999. More and more programs are being formed across the country to give kids the opportunity to play soccer. The stars of the future are just beginning to learn how to play this great game. They might break the greatest records in this sport one day if they work hard enough!

Soccer is an international sport, so the stars of tomorrow are practicing their skills in countries all around the world!

GLOSSARY

achieve: To get by effort.

alternate: To take turns.

aspire: To work to get something high or great.

award: To give something good.

competitive: Done with the purpose of winning.

dribble: To run while moving the ball forward with the feet.

eliminate: To remove from future competition because of a loss.

international: Involving two or more countries.

opposing: Belonging to the other team in a game.

preliminary: Coming before the main part.

professional: Having to do with a job someone does for a living.

statistic: A number that stands for a piece of information.

tournament: A contest or series of contests played for a championship.

INDEX

WEBSITES

Due to the changing nature of Internet links, PowerKids Press has developed
an online list of websites related to the subject of this book. This site is updated
regularly. Please use this link to access the list: www.powerkidslinks.com/gris/soc